Ants Will Not Eat Your Fingers

ANTS WILL NOT
EAT YOUR FINGERS

A Selection of Traditional African Poems

Edited by
Leonard W. Doob

WALKER AND COMPANY
New York

Published in the United States of America by Walker and Company, a division of the Walker Publishing Company, Inc.

Published in Canada by The Ryerson Press, Toronto.

Library of Congress Catalog Card Number: 66-22514

Printed in the United States of America

Designed by Lena Fong Lueg

I salute you,
Magnificent Africa —
A russet landscape,
Gay, gloomy,
Powerful, weak,
Rooted, youthful —
With your own creations

Preface

This book has a very serious purpose: it would provoke mirth and give pause by means of poems that can be immediately understood and appreciated without an explanatory text or footnotes. It makes no trivial claim that the verses are typical of the society from which, out of context, they have been ripped; that the societies are representative of sub-Saharan Africa; or that the translations are faithful or scholarly. It has no thesis, it would prove nothing.

How, then, have the poems been selected? The reply must be that while reading books, monographs, and journals on Africa for presumably scholarly reasons during the last decade or so, I have stumbled upon passages which have struck me as being actually or potentially poetic; and more recently I have sought out such passages. A single criterion, consequently, has guided me to the poems for the volume: I like them, whether or not I believe that they reflect a sentiment or experience shared by all men on all continents and in every age.

Almost without exception a few words or phrases in each selection have been altered, more often omitted, and less frequently added. These changes are not indicated for, it is hoped, a very acceptable reason: I have tried desperately, conscientiously to retain the spirit or essence of the poem and even perhaps to improve its power to convey that message. The typography has been ruthlessly standardized.

By and large the poems are traditional in three senses. They have been attributed to no known or knowable creators by their discoverers who have stated or implied that they are—or once were—part of the ritual of the society. Then, secondly, they have been relatively uninfluenced by European or Eastern poetic traditions. Finally, unlike poems in our society, which are generally appreciated only by a segregated elite taking pride in their own sensitivity, these poems are likely to be so embedded in an African ceremony or tradition that they affect almost every member of the group without being recognized as a separate genre; many are supposed to be sung or chanted; and most deal with the eternal themes of love, death, jealousy, anxiety, and—oh, I must stop, for I have vowed not to make this preface sound misleadingly anthropological or psychological.

The order of presentation is alphabetical by society or tribe. I have supplied mildly expository and reasonably accurate titles. The name of the translator from the original African language appears at the bottom of each selection; an asterisk after that name signifies that someone else—more frequently than not, the person perforce is I—has translated that translation into English. To discover the precise source of the first translator or to identify the second one, when it is not I, the eager or perverse reader need only consult the references at the end of the volume.

I alone am completely and proudly responsible for all decisions and for all errors and distortions. Quite obviously I mean that admission to be neither perfunctory nor apologetic. I declare deep or appropriate gratitude to the Africans who, deliberately or not, composed the verses long ago; to the travelers, missionaries, colonial officials, and the scholarly Africans and Europeans who transcribed and translated them later on; to Wolf Leslau, in one of whose sensitive translations, as can be noted on page 53, the title for the present collection has been discerned; and to the publishers who gra-

8

ciously granted permission to quote what I have chosen to quote. The collecting and editing of these fragments, perhaps because I have been driven by avocational, profound, and unconscious interests, has been very, very gratifying. I hope Africans and non-Africans can now have equally satisfying, though different experiences from reading them. They, too, must be striving to grasp the frail and vigorous emotions which, I guess, poetry and people would always express and evoke.

L. W. D.

Battle Hymn

We are poured on the enemy like a mighty torrent:
We are poured like a river in spate
When the rain is in the mountains.
The water hisses down the sands, swirling, exultant
And the tree that stood in its path is torn up quivering,
It is tossed from eddy to eddy.
We are poured on the enemy
And they are bewildered:
They look this way and that seeking escape,
But our spears fall thickly about them.
Our spears cling to their bodies
And they are routed.
They look this way and that for deliverance,
But they cannot escape us,
The avengers, the great killers.

J. H. Driberg

1.

If you are hungry, cook yourself a meal,
Why do you cry?
You are the child of a yam farmer,
Why do you cry?
You are the child of a cocoyam farmer,
Why do you cry?

2.

Someone would like to have you for her child,
But you are my own.
Someone wishes she had you to nurse on a good mat,
Someone wishes you were hers.
She would put you on a camel blanket,
But I have you to rear on a torn mat.
Someone wishes she had you,
But it is I who have you.

J. H. Kwabena Nketia

A Song of the Minstrels   *Akan*

She is standing at the crossroads hawking onions.
She is sitting at the great crossroads hawking onions.
When you go in the morning,
Give my greetings to her
And to her husband
Whose adultery fee is outrageous.

J. B. Danquah

Dancing Song   *Akan*

Young lady,
Look for some medicine:
You have been ill too long.
Get yourself some medicine,
So that someone will marry you.

J. H. Kwabena Nketia

1.

I sleep long and soundly,
Suddenly the door creaks,
Confused, I open my eyes,
And find my love standing there:
What matters death to me?

2.

It has been raining and raining,
It has been raining and raining,
I go out to leave my footprints:
I see the footprints of my love.
All footprints are not alike:
I go out to leave my footprints
And find the footprints of my love.

3.

He has two loves,
He has two loves,
I go to see him off.
I meet the other woman.
I cannot go on,
I cannot go back,
I burst into tears.

J. H. Kwabena Nketia

Elegy for Duodu, a Brave Man   *Akan*

Duodu, the King's servant,
Who was killed through his valor:
See, the rain washes his house away.
Duodu, I am grieved by your death.
Alas it has always been so:
Once dead, you are useless,
And all is decay.

J. H. Kwabena Nketia

Evaluation   *Akan*

It is man who counts.
I call upon gold:
It answers not.
I call upon drapery:
It answers not.
It is man who counts.

J. G. Christaller

Song for an Absent Chief   *Akan*

How cold is an empty room,
How sad a deserted house,
O, how melancholic is an empty room,
I roam around looking, looking.

J. H. Kwabena Nketia

1.

Hunters, you have slept,
Rise up you hunters,
You who lie till dawn,
Let us sing with affection,
Let us make offerings,
The spirits have come.

2.

You follow the wild pig,
I shall follow the hartebeest.
You follow the wild pig,
I shall follow the hartebeest.
It is good to chase the big game with horns.

3.

My wife, grind meal,
Tomorrow I shall journey
To reach the game herds,
I shall not return until I tire:
Sing cheerfully,
I am a wild dog
Which chases and chases.

It is boiling and boiling,
The hunters are cooking in a big pot.
It is boiling and boiling,
The hunters are cooking in a big pot.
It is really boiling hard,
I must kill two head tomorrow.

5.

Heavens, my heart is throbbing,
While I see them standing.
Heavens, my heart is throbbing,
While I see them standing,
While I see the game standing.

B. Stefaniszyn

17

When I asked for him at Entoto, he was towards Akaki,
So they told me;
When I asked for him at Akaki, he was towards Jarer,
So they told me;
When I asked for him at Jarer, he was at Mendar,
So they told me;
When I asked for him at Mendar, he was towards Awash,
So they told me;
When I asked for him at Awash, he was towards Chercher,
So they told me;
When I asked for him at Chercher, he was towards Harar,
So they told me;
When I asked for him at Harar, he was towards Djibouti,
So they told me;
When I asked for him at Djibouti, he had crossed the sea,
Or so they said:
I sent to find him a hundred times,
But I never found him.
I sit by the fire and weep:
What a fool he is
To hope he will ever find anyone to equal me.

Sylvia Pankhurst

Antiphony

1.

(1st Woman)

My husband likes me too much,
He is good to me,
But I am not able to like him;
And so I listen to my lover.

2.

(1st Man)

My wife does not please,
I have grown tired of her;
And so I shall favor myself with another
Who is very beautiful.

3.

(2nd Woman)

My lover tempts me with sweet words,
But my husband is always good to me;
And so I must like him well,
Also I must be true to him.

4.

(2nd Man)

Girl, you are more beautiful than my wife,
But wife is not what I would call you;
For a wife pleases only her husband
And you, when I leave you, you go to others.

T. Edward Bowdich

19

Chant for Girls
During Puberty Ceremony

We play and dance for you
That you may remain with us,
That you may bear ten children,
That no bad thing may come upon you.
Let the elephant give you her womb
That you may bear ten children.
Long live the people of your village,
Long live your relatives and elders
Who celebrate this festival for you.

R. S. *Rattray*

Perspective

I lie on my back
Looking upwards;
Even so, I do not see the Supreme Being.
What, then, do you expect
When you sprawl there on your belly?

R. S. Rattray

Bangi

Songs Before
Clitoridectomy Rites

—

1.

(By the female elder who officiates)
Once we were playmates
But today I take command over you,
For, you see, I am a man,
I have a knife in my hand
And I am going to operate upon you.
Your clitoris which you guard so jealously
I shall cut off
And cast upon the ground,
For today I am a man.
I have a cold, cold heart,
Otherwise I could not operate upon you.
Afterwards your wound will be dressed,
And I shall be aware of many things:
I shall know who takes care of herself
And who does not.

2.

(By those about to be initiated)
Your words produce great fear within us,
But we cannot run off.
Yet you, you once were also an initiate
And obviously you are not the least bit dead:
So we too shall not die.

3.

(By one of the initiates)

Do not speak thus, my sisters,
My heart is much too heavy
And my fear is great.
Ah, if I could change myself into a bird,
Oh, I would fly away quickly.

4.

(By another)

To be afraid is disgraceful,
So much the worse if we die,
We must be brave.

5.

(By all)

Today I am going to be an initiate,
I shall leave the house of my mother,
I shall no longer see
Either my father or my brothers:
Who then will bring them water?
Who will prepare their meals?
Who will sweep their house?

*A. M. Vergiat**

Songs During Circumcision
Rites of Boys

1.

(Before the operation)

Today is a great day
For us, the youth.
Among us no girl can be found,
We have nothing to do with love today.

Tonight our sweetheart will be alone in her house.
Whoever lay down in the village
Will sleep tonight in the forest,
And the beloved will cry for her lover.

2.

(After the operation)

Once I said, "There are no initiates,"
But now I have seen the knife.
I have seen the knife and I was not afraid,
For, when the knife cuts, that is good,
If it does not cut, that is not good,
For all men would jeer at you
And say that you are like a woman.

Once when I went hunting,
The men laughed at me,
But now they will no longer jeer at me.

Young boys are not circumcised,
But you, you are now one of the elect,
You will no longer be their comrade,
For I would be ashamed of you.

*A. M. Vergiat**

Basari   Lullaby

Be still, my child,
Do you see those birds
In the tree?
If you cry,
A little bird
Is going to carry you off.

*Ch. Béart**

Bemba   Initiation Song of Girls

The man is the peak of the house;
That is what we have understood.
It is women who make the pinnacle
On top of the roof.

Audrey I. Richards

26

Hunting Prayer *Bushmen*

I do not know
What will happen to me
Regarding food,
What will happen to me,
Regarding food.
I do not know
What I shall do
To get something to eat.
Let us eat and become big.

*Viktor Lebzelter**

Bushmen The Sun's Curse Upon the Horse
(uncertain)

From now on your time of dying is certain,
This is your curse, your time of dying is certain.
And you will eat both day and night
Without satisfying the desire of your heart,
Even though you graze till dawn
And then again till dusk.
Behold, this judgment I pass upon you.

James A. Honey

Prayer to the Star Canopus

Bushmen

O Star coming there,
Let me see a springbok.
O Star coming there,
Let me dig out ants' food
With this stick.
O Star coming there,
Let me dig out ants' food
With this stick.

O Star coming there,
Let me see a springbok tomorrow,
O Star coming there,
I give you my heart,
Do give me your heart.

O Star coming there,
May I see a proteles tomorrow,
Let the dog kill it,
Let me eat it,
Let me eat, filling my body,
That I may lie and sleep at night.

Dorothea F. Bleek

Central Bantu
(unspecified)

Song for the Lazy

If you are hungry
Use your hoe,
The only drug
The doctors know.

Dugald Campbell

Chaga

Children's Song

A bird once took wing,
Alighted in our green, green land,
Quickly burst forth in song:
"What a beautiful, beautiful country."
But shortly after nesting in our grove,
He fell ill,
Forthwith destroyed what he had built.
"What an evil, evil country,"
He then sang out
And flew away back to the steppes.

*Bruno Gutmann**

Morning Prayer *Chaga*

O Great Mountain, you chief,
I recline, I am a gnat
But I would like to get up
And be an elephant.
O Sun, you chief,
Even as the Mountain remains immutable,
Your life undergoes no change.
Come, burst forth,
Let me shine like you, O chief.

*Bruno Gutmann**

Tributes to the Chief

1.

Riches galore are found at the chief's headquarters.
Open the door,
There enter the cows and the goats
That seek and love you.

2.

Into what would I like to change myself?
Into the knife with which the chief cuts his meat.
What would I like to become?
The cup from which the chief drinks beer.

3.

If you separate yourself from this bountiful source,
What would you eat?
If you separate yourself from the chief,
What would you eat?
What you would eat would be the knots of branches
And the bark of ghastly trees.

Bruno Gutmann*

Chorus Sung by
Co-Wives to One Another

Dahomeans

Woman, your soul is misshapen,
In haste was it made;
So fleshless a face speaks,
Saying your soul was formed without care.
The ancestral clay for your making
Was molded in haste.
A thing of no beauty are you,
Your face unsuited for a face,
Your feet unsuited for feet.

*Melville J. Herskovits**

I see it,
There is no enjoying beyond death.
And I say to you all,
That which your senses taste of life
Goes with you.

I say to you,
The wives you have,
The passion you know of them,
Goes with you.

I say to you,
The meats you eat,
The relish you have of them,
Goes with you.

I say to you,
The drinks you drink,
The pleasure of them,
Goes with you.

I say to you,
The pipes you smoke,
The quiet they bring,
Goes with you.

Come, then,
Dance all the colors of life
For a lover of pleasure
Now dead.

Frances Herskovits

Ditty for a Child
Losing His First Tooth

Dahomeans

He who has lost a tooth,
Cannot eat salt:
Come, give me palm oil
To eat with my cake.

I do not want the teeth of a pig,
They are big.
I want the teeth of a goat,
They are small.

Melville J. Herskovits

The Giver of Life
Placed the sun in great space,
And said: No hand
Shall be the length to reach it;
Though clouds disappear,
And we become a mountain,
Immovable and high,
It will not be that the hand obeys not.

The Giver of Life
Placed the sun in the heavens,
And said: No eye
Shall have the cunning to see within;
Though clouds disappear,
And we become a mountain,
Immovable and high,
It will not be that the eye obeys not.

Frances Herskovits

Hymn of Propitiation *Didinga*

White cow of heaven, you have fed in rich pastures
And you who were small have grown great.
White cow of heaven, your horns have curved full circle
And are joined as one.
White cow of heaven, we throw at you the dust
Which your feet have trampled in our kraals.
White cow of heaven, give your blessing on the kraals
Which you have overseen
So that the udders of our cows may be heavy
And that our women may rejoice.

J. H. Driberg

Didinga   Song for Dance of Young Girls

We mold a pot as our mothers did.
The pot, where is the pot?
The pot, it is here.
We mold the pot as our mothers did.

First, the base of the pot.
Strip by strip, and layer by layer.
Supple fingers kneading the clay,
Long fingers molding the clay,
Stiff thumbs shaping the clay,
Layer by layer and strip by strip,
We build up the pot of our mother.

We build up the pot of our mother,
Strip by strip and layer by layer.
Its belly swells like the paunch of a hyena,
Of a hyena which has eaten a whole sheep.
Its belly swells like a mother of twins.
It is a beautiful pot, the pot of our mother.
It swells like a mother of twins.

J. H. Driberg

War Song

Dinka

Though the tribe holds a feast against me,
I shall not fear;
Though all the people hold a feast against me,
I shall not fear;
O my tribe, I am a bull with sharpened horns,
I am a maddened bull.

Godfrey Lienhardt

1.

God has really put an end to mankind this year,
O misery, O misery.
He has snatched away our leaders this year,
O misery.
He has snatched away our elders this year,
O misery.
He has even snatched away young people this year,
O misery.

2.

O Death, what have you now contrived,
O Ancestral Gods, what have you done now?
Even when you have approached us face-to-face,
You then also come at us from the rear.
O Death, what have you now contrived,
You have made me into a worthless blade of corn,
O Ancestral Gods, what have you done now?

3.

Since the beginning of time,
A natural death has been our destiny,
Yes, all men must die;
They must yield to fate.
Man, nevertheless, does not yield,
His struggles make no sense,
For God in heaven is invisible and awesome.

Friedrich Ebding*

Lamentation

I would know nothing of customs
That I do not recognize,
Tell me nothing about uncertain matters.
If the heart suffers a blow,
Then man complains.
But if it is filled with joy,
Let him burst into song.
I would know nothing of customs
That I do not recognize,
Tell me nothing about uncertain matters.

*Johannes Ittmann**

1.

I do not wish to have anything more to do with women:
Should I put on a collar and wear shoes?
Beauty, your kind of beauty,
Leaves me unmoved.
What should I do with beauty?
Beauty, your kind of beauty,
You keep it for yourself.

2.

Love is a thin thread:
If wind blows over it,
Then, lo, it breaks.
So take care,
If the thread of love is torn,
It can never be tied again.

3.

Tell the young people today:
You cannot simply marry a woman when you wish.
To acquire a bride, that is a matter of money;
To marry, that is a matter of money;
To take a wife, that is a matter of money.

*Paul Wiegräbe**

Dolor

1.

The fine place for playing quickly falls to ruin,
The fine place of enjoyment quickly falls to ruin,
The thick virgin forest turns easily to grassland,
Our beautiful town becomes grassland again.
Our beautiful home becomes grassland again.

2.

May the gravediggers not bury me,
May the gravediggers not bury me,
Let them bury my feet
But leave my body free,
That my friends may come to see my face,
That they may come and look upon my face.

Diedrich Westermann

1.

We wish to be joyful,
While we live, we wish to be joyful,
For in the grave we have nothing,
While we live, we wish to be joyful.
If I knew what to do
To ask for life,
Then I would ask for life.
If I had good palm wine to sacrifice,
Then I would go to the shrine of God
To beg for life;
If I had good water as a gift,
Then I would go to the shrine of the gods
To beg for life.

2.

Death sits on a tree in the village;
Mother, hide your child, something has happened.
Death sits on a tree in the village,
Mother, hide your child, something has happened.
Recently, as dawn came, Death took a club under his arm,
Death will truly slay someone again.
The plan which Death has now conceived
No man can know;
The plan which Death has now conceived
No man can know.

*Paul Wiegräbe**

Yearning

Mother dear,
Mother, who freely gives of what she has:
Fresh food and cooked meals alike.
Mother, who never deserts the hearth,
Mother, hearken to me!
The crying child will call after its mother.
How is it that mother does not answer me when I call?
Are we quarreling?

Geormbeeyi Adali-Mortti

Fang   Distracting an Opponent
                           in a Game of Skill

You really resemble
An old man who has no teeth
And who wants to eat elephant hide,
Or a woman without a backside
Who sits down on a hard wooden stool.
You also resemble a stupid dolt
Who while hunting lets an antelope pass by
And knows that his father is sick at home.

*Günter Tessmann**

Invocation to
the Spirit of the Race

Fang

In you the last returns to the first,
The first returns to the last.
And in common accord,
Your breath that does not die
Reunites them all,
Your breath reunites them
Without ever wearying.
It makes an unending whole
And future children,
Offspring of our race,
Will also be your children, O father,
As I today am your child.

*R. P. H. Trilles**

If a jackal bothers you, show him a hyena,
If a hyena bothers you, show him a lion,
If a lion bothers you, show him an elephant,
If an elephant bothers you, show him a hunter,
If a hunter bothers you, show him a snake,
If a snake bothers you, show him a stick,
If a stick bothers you, show it a fire,
If a fire bothers you, show it a river,
If a river bothers you, show it a wind,
If a wind bothers you, show it God.

D. W. Arnott

Blessings Upon an Infant   *Ga*

Hail, let happiness come:
The stranger has arrived,
His back is towards the darkness,
His face is towards the light.

May he work for his father,
May he work for his mother,
May he not steal,
May he not be wicked.

The children of this family
Forgive everything that can be forgiven.
May he eat by the work of his five fingers,
May he come to respect the world.

Upon his mother's head, Life.
Upon his father's head, Life.
If we should join up to make a circle,
May our chain be complete.
If we dig a well,
May we come upon water.
If we draw water to bathe our joints,
May they be refreshed.

Hail, let happiness come.
Are our voices one?
Hail, let happiness come.

M. J. Field

Ganda   In Honor of a King
                    Who Acquired Several Young Wives

For me I shall buy an elderly one who will feed me,
For me I shall buy an elderly one who will feed me,
Because the young ones belong to the king.

                                        Apolo Kagwa*

Maternal Advise to Young Parrots   *Ganda*

Never get up till the sun gets up,
Or the mists will give you a cold.
And a parrot whose lungs have once been touched
Will never live to be old.

Never eat plums that are not quite ripe,
For perhaps they will give you a pain;
And never dispute what a hornbill says
Or you will never dispute again.

Never despise the power of speech;
Learn every word as it comes.
For this is the pride of the parrot race,
That it speaks in a hundred tongues.

Never stay up when the sun goes down,
But sleep in your own home bed.
And if you have been good, as a parrot should,
You will dream that your tail is red.

Akiki K. Nyabongo

Ghanaians
(unspecified)

Song of the Turtle

We lived in freedom
Before man appeared:
Our world was undisturbed,
One day followed the other joyfully,
Dissent was never heard.

Then man broke into our forest
With cunning and belligerence,
He pursued us
With greed and envy:
Our freedom vanished.

*Mike Joslin**

The Farmer

You who cultivate fields,
Your merit is great,
Wealth flows from your fingers,
The sea gushes out in front of your house.
You share what you produce
With the begging cripple at your door:
For this you receive blessing.
You share what you produce
With the begging orphan at your door:
For this you receive blessing.
And so ants will not eat your fingers;
After you die, your destiny will be paradise,
As long as you live, you will be blessed.

Wolf Leslau

Wail of One Rejected

Sweet, listen to me, I entreat you:
When I look you in the eye,
I seem to be losing my sanity,
The skin of my body grows numb,
All my thoughts involve only you —
I crave you, yet you feel no passion.
Your father stops me from courting you.
Hence I shall set out for the King's palace,
And ride away to war,
For on account of you I would die.

*Rudolf Prietze**

Praise Song for a Drummer *Hausa*

The drum drums health,
The drum drums wealth,
He takes his wife six hundred thousand cowries.
The drum drums health,
The drum drums wealth,
He takes his son six hundred thousand cowries,
The drum drums health,
The drum drums wealth.

Mary Smith

Song *Hima*

To become a chief's favorite
Is not always comfortable;
It is like making friends
With a hippopotamus.

Hugh Tracey

Hlubi   Girl's Song

Come, it is late in the day:
All those of my age are married,
And now I wander, wander all alone.
Hold back the sun that it may not go down
Without carrying the news of my bethrothal.

A. C. Jordan

Hottentots   Civil War Song

"Be so good, my brother,
Be so friendly,
Allow me to drink from this water hole."
"Lay down your arms
And then drink water."
"I shall not lay them down."

Leonhard Schultze°

Love Song   *Hottentots*

I shall never win you,
I shall never win you,
I shall never win you.

*Leonhard Schultze**

To Doves   *Hurutshe*

Coo-coo-roo of the girls,
Hopper in the sand;
They are playing behind the kraal,
They make short turns and little circles,
They make short turns and little circles again and again;
Coo-coo-roo, coo-coo-roo, coo-coo-roo-coo-coo.

D. F. v. d. Merwe

Love Song for Nneka
(Whose Name Means "Mother's Love Is Best")

Nneka, lovely damsel,
Beautiful Nneka;
Your teeth are as white as pearls,
Beautiful Nneka.

Nneka with body like bronze,
Beautiful Nneka;
Your hair is black and glossy,
Beautiful Nneka.

Nneka, lovely as the pelican,
Beautiful Nneka;
Nneka, I love you so,
Beautiful Nneka.

D. C. Osadebay

On Truth

One thread of truth in a shuttle
Will weave a hundred threads of lies.
Vomiting one's liver cures the most severe biliousness;
The hatching of an egg is unpleasant for the shell:
Do not match yourself against Providence.
God is all-powerful:
He prevents the eye from seeing the eyelashes.
Eggs become lice:
The small man becomes the great man.
Stick to the truth:
Truth is like the light of dawn,
Untruthfulness is like darkness at sunset.

J. R. Patterson

Praise Songs for
Various Chiefs and Sultans

1.

Hail all powerful,
Today you are the world's health-giver,
You hold destiny in your hands,
Today you have made the world a paradise.
Send out the heat of your fiery spirit:
No one can oppose your plans;
You are one for whom a male goat and a bull give milk;
You are the only good man I have seen since my birth.

2.

Son of a man invincible:
Just as the remedy
For hot food is a calabash spoon;
And for the dangers of water, a canoe;
And for being seized with hunger, a milch cow;
And for cold, a blanket;
And for protection against a tornado, a large leather sheet,
So you, son of man invincible, are the remedy
Against all that annoys.

3.

Alone you are equal to a thousand men,
You can run hither and yon like a puppy;
You have the patience of a male pelican;
You are like boneless flesh and like brains;
Your eye is to be feared as an elephant hunter's spear;
Your eyelashes are like arrows.

4.

May God preserve you in the same way,
As He does not allow friendship to grow old;
Your bounty is to us as the milk of a cow
Which never grows dry for the calf at its side;
From you we find our food in the evening,
And water to drink in the morning:
May God grant that we may see you every day,
For to see you is to see the world filled with light
And to attain one's desire.
May long life, good fortune, perfect health be yours:
Reign amidst happiness.

J. R. Patterson

Kgatla   Lullaby of an
                         Abandoned Mother

Hush, my forgotten one,
Hush, my child;
These labors of love
You have given me,
For the heart eats what is beloved
But rejects what is bestowed.

I. Schapera

Army Song   *Kipsigi*

Mother of children, mother of children:
Put the fire near the pot,
The army is going to war, oo wo ho.
Repair the bridge:
The men must pass,
The cattle they capture must pass,
The army is going to war, oo wo ho.
Praise the warriors,
They are like elephants:
When there is a scare,
They kneel on one foot and hide
From the enemy and then, and then
When he comes they stand up and roar
And terrify his heart, oo wo ho.
Wife of my brother,
Press food into the bag of war,
File me the spear,
Rub it with fat,
To kill Masai, Kisii, and Luo,
To drive away their cattle,
Their brown cattle with tails white tipped.
The army is going to war, oo wo ho.

J. G. Peristiany

You shake the waist — we shake.
Let us shake the waist — we shake.
You shake the waist — we shake.
I am going to my lover — we shake.
Even if it is raining — we shake —
I am going to my lover — we shake.
I am going to my lover — we shake.
He is at Chesumei — we shake.
Even when night comes — we shake —
I am going to my lover — we shake.
Even if he hits me — we shake —
I am going at night — we shake.
Even if there is a wild animal — we shake —
I am going to my lover — we shake.
A person not knowing a lover — we shake —
Knows nothing at all — we shake.

J. G. Peristiany

Hymn to God *Kongo*

The elder takes all that he can,
The young man does the same,
But above all men a great God reigns.
If we fish only once,
That means hunger.
If we draw wine from a single palm tree,
That means thirst.
Ancestors come to eat with us,
But death which will eat us
Does not eat with man;
Death wanders in deep valleys,
In very distant lands.

*J. Van Wing**

Incantation During Initiation
into a Secret Society

O High Spirit, listen, father:
Whoever betrays our secret,
Twist his neck, eat his flesh,
For it is your flesh, O Master;
Goad him so that he will die far away,
Drink his blood, O Master.

If a candidate does not complete the initiation this month,
Send him back to his village,
Follow him, twist his neck,
Then he will realize that he must bring it to an end.

But the child who recognizes me,
Respect him,
Fill his house with joy,
Do not bend his backbone;
Then in good time he will have children
Overflowing with vigor.

*J. Van Wing**

Rain-Making Litany

Lango

We must overcome the east wind
Which brings no rain;
We crave rain,
Let showers pour,
Let rain fall;
If rain comes, then all is well.

If it rains and grain ripens, then all is well;
If children rejoice, then all is well;
If women rejoice, then all is well;
If young men sing, then all is well;
If the aged rejoice, then all is well;
If rain comes, then all is well.

May the wind veer to the south,
So that the torrents will flow;
May our grain fill the granaries,
May the granaries overflow;
If rain comes, then all is well;
If rain comes, then all is well.

J. H. Driberg

1.

The rhinoceros is at silent rest,
The rhinoceros stands
At the foot of the acacia
And is utterly silent.

2.

O dappled hyena, O dappled hyena,
What do you seek here,
Do you seek the rhinoceros
That throws up dust?

3.

The reedbuck stands on the ant hill,
It stands there unwavering
And calls to the cob
Like a young man.

4.

In the banana leaves,
In the banana leaves of Olum,
The leopard sleeps,
Let us go and see him.

5.

The serval and the meerkat,
They travel by night,
They take the chicken
And drive off the cow.

6.

The buffalo goes with head on high,
The bird is on his ear,
The flute of the buffalo
Sounds in the river.

J. H. Driberg

Prayer to Ancestral Spirits *Logoli*

We have placed you in the earth for good:
May you rest there in peace,
And may we who have stayed behind
Live in peace.
May you bless the children
Whom you have left behind,
May they perform their work well.
We pray to you,
You cannot say we have forgotten you.

Günter Wagner

When a son leaves our womb,
We are joyously glad;
The gladness heals us.
When he leaves our larger womb,
The village, we lie torn, bleeding:
There is no healing, no healing
Until a son returns to us,
There is no healing;
Only when he returns
Can there be healing.
Oh, oh, our sons,
Stay with us now
Until we come together
In the town of the Dead.

Esther Warner

Hain-Teny (Love Poem) *Malagasy*

I represent the eyes,
You the ears:
You listen to me,
I look at you.
I am the bird-trap
You the piaster-pieces:
If you abandon me,
The weight can only break loose;
Should I abandon you,
You will rust.

Miriam Koshland

Malagasy   A Love Message

Longing pleases me like sweet fragrance,
Memory brings me pain.
I dreamt of a young man
Who would come to admire me
And not of a handsome stranger
Who would smile at me and pass by.

*Flavien Ranaivo**

Masai   Proverb

The stranger
With his belly full of good food
Runs to a woman,
While you
With only a scrap of wood to gnaw
Must drag along your saucepan.

*Blaise Cendrars**

Song to a Gun Masai

For you alone, O gun, for you alone,
In the depths of the woods,
Far, far away, I have marched long in the forest,
Hearing no more the barking dogs;
No longer hearing them,
Nor the cocks that love noise,
No more the cocks.
Going far away from the scolding women,
Going far from their dark huts.

*Blaise Cendrars**

Masemola

Formulas Recited as Divinations After Throwing Four Principal and Forty-Two Accessory Bones

1.

(Foretelling hardship)

The voice of an expectant mother:
I want to speak and cannot speak,
I want to hear and cannot hear,
I want to find and cannot find,
I strain my eyes to look for food,
But all in vain, they see no food.

2.

(Diagnosing pregnancy)

They speak of pain and suffering,
Of illness that is coming soon.
She trembles now with pain,
Her stomach has never felt such agony,
The pangs of childbirth tear her womb.
You son of a mighty warrior,
This is between the two of you,
Between husband and wife
To give and take in secrecy.

3.

(Foretelling murder or poisoning)

A hidden wound, a secret crime:
A spear is cutting up my bowels,
The blood unseen is streaming round.
It is pointless to try to flee:
My fate already has been sealed.

4.

(Foretelling the punishment of the guilty)
Your turn has come, O fierce leopard,
Your turn to be the prey, to feel the pain.
You will be dragged to death today,
Even as you have dragged many others.

5.

(Warning against arrogance)
This points to those who rob and covet:
Beware, you herdsmen of cattle,
These cows you drive out to pasture,
Do not belong to you, you must remember,
You may not even drink their milk.

W. M. Eiselen

Chaff is in my eye,
A crocodile has me by the leg,
A goat is in the garden,
A porcupine is cooking in the pot,
Meal is drying on the pounding rock,
The King has summoned me to court,
And I must go to the funeral of my mother-in-law:
In short, I am busy.

Merlin Ennis

Song of the Fishermen

Mbundu

O fish, come
And take your good food.
Do not send the little fish
To spoil the good food.
Better you come
And take the good food
With all your strength.

Wilfrid Dyson Hambly

There are, some people say, no riches in the bush.
But look at an ant hill:
It has a helmet providing shelter from the rain.
See that beetle:
His coat does not go around him
And yet it has three buttons.
A bird which lives there in the bush
Has a wooden house:
Who is the carpenter?
This bush cow wears boots
Like those of a soldier;
That baboon has a black coat
Like a policeman;
And the kingfisher has a silk gown.
Why, then, do some people say
There are no riches in the bush?

K. L. Little

On Wealth

I am rich
And I shall die;
You are poor
And you will die.

F. W. H. Migeod

Mongo   From the Legend
of the National Hero

1.

Father, send back this woman,
Send her back quickly.
Her figure is not beautiful,
She does not know how to behave herself,
She acts like a fool.
Father, send back this woman.

2.

Monkeys, climb up the rubber trees,
And eat the fruit.
Elephants, leave the pools,
Attack the young palm trees
And eat out their cores.
Boars, by the light of the moon,
Run across the fields of manioc,
Ravage them and eat away your hunger.
Parrots, with outstretched wings,
Fly to the palm grove,
Skip from branch to branch
And satiate yourself upon the fruits,
For I am going into combat with Sausau, the Murderer.

3.

We are alone, all alone,
Nobody wants to marry us.
We are worthy of pity,
For men turn away from us.
Why this contempt which hurts us?
Why this scorn which pains us?
Are we less beautiful?
Are we less robust?
Are we less industrious?
Let us weed our fields,
Let us pound manioc,
Our solitude will come to an end.

4.

Sun, rise again from where you come,
Once more begin your journey,
Resume your place in the firmament,
For I need your brightness.
I cannot do battle in darkness,
Help me to light my way faithfully.

*Joseph Esser**

Songs During Love Dances

1.

My husband, keep me well,
Keep me in proper fashion:
A woman ages as quickly as okra.

2.

You admire this girl,
Her beauty has won you
And you will not let her go.
Are you perchance this child's mother or father?
You are not the God who created her.

*A. A. D. Delobsom**

Dance Tune

Ngoni

My wife is very bad,
She looks this way and that.

Hans Koritschoner

Lullaby

Ngoni

Hush, my child,
Never mind, never mind.
Hush, my child,
Never mind, never mind.
There is a busybody gossiping,
There is a busybody gossiping.
Ho! we reap the maize.

Margaret Read

Listen, O earth. We shall mourn because of you.
Listen, O earth. Shall we all die on the earth?

The earth does not get fat,
It makes an end of those who wear the head plumes.
We shall die on the earth.
The earth does not get fat,
It makes an end of those who act swiftly as heroes.
Shall we die on the earth?

The earth does not get fat;
It makes an end of the chiefs.
Shall we all die on the earth?
The earth does not get fat,
It makes an end of the women chiefs.
Shall we die on the earth?

The earth does not get fat,
It makes an end of the nobles.
Shall we die on the earth?
The earth does not get fat,
It makes an end of the royal women.
Shall we die on the earth?

The earth does not get fat,
It makes an end of the common people.

Shall we die on the earth?
The earth does not get fat,
It makes an end of all the beasts.
Shall we die on the earth?

Listen, you who are asleep,
Who are left tightly closed in the land,
Shall we all sink into the earth?
Listen, O earth, the sun is setting tightly,
We shall all enter into the earth.

Margaret Read

Ngwaketse   Praise for a Chief

Elephant of the yellowwood trees, trumpet,
Let your voice pass over Dilolo Hills
And be heard also at Ramoutsa;
Let them fear and cast their children into the hearths
When they hear the All-Conquering trumpeting.

I. Schapera

Nyamwezi   Hunter's Song

In the bush, in the deep forest,
We do our work;
One hunter digs a hole,
The other sets a trap.
We divide the meat with our followers,
Another part we cut in pieces
And dry over the fire.
We all die in the same way;
And so, hunters, let us be good comrades.

Hans Koritschoner

Prayer for Rain   *Nyanja*

This little cloud, and this,
This little cloud, and this,
Let the rains come
With this little cloud.
Give us water,
Our hearts are dry,
O Lord,
Give us water,
Our hearts are dry,
O Lord.

R. S. Rattray

There death now has come to the homestead,
Enter not, my brother,
Ho-ya-ho-ya-ho.
A maiden, alas, there is sleeping,
Ho-ya-ho-ya-ho.

Her rest is dark and unending,
She returns no more,
Ho-ya-ho-ya-ho.
Her spirit has passed on a journey,
Ho-ya-ho-ya-ho.

Ella Kidney

Dance of the Animals   *Pygmie.*

I throw myself to the left,
I turn myself to the right,
I am the fish
Who glides in the water, who glides,
Who twists himself, who leaps.
Everything lives, everything dances, everything sings.

The bird flies,
Flies, flies, flies,
Goes, comes back, passes,
Mounts, hovers, and drops down.
I am the bird.
Everything lives, everything dances, everything sings.

The monkey, from bough to bough,
Runs, leaps, and jumps,
With his wife, with his little one,
His mouth full, his tail in the air:
This is the monkey, this is the monkey.
Everything lives, everything dances, everything sings.

*Blaise Cendrars**

Rangi   Song During Circumcision Rite

Hunger is bad,
Hunger is like a lion,
Hunger is bad,
It makes us eat locusts.

H. A. Fosbrooke

Sandawe   Song for a Dance

Night time my Melenga
Boldly undresses at the well.
"Here I am quite saucy,
Ha ha, I can strut about."

Night time, grandmother, father,
She suddenly swaggers out,
"I am Melenga,
Are you my father?"

Otto Dempwolff

A Boast of the Mad Mullah
Who Fought the British

Somali

No man exists
Who can lay hold of a wild elephant
And lead him around;
No man exists
Who can grip a lion by the nape of the neck
And give him a punch:
So is it with reference to the Mullah.

Enrico Cerulli

As day on the edge of night
And night on the edge of day,
So is the spirit of man
When he reaches
The gates of maturity.
The zenith of thought,
The equilibrium of the spiritual
With the physical.

Somali Ministry of Information

Love Lyrics   *Somali*

1.

I long for you, as one
Whose dhow in summer winds
Is blown adrift and lost,
Longs for land, and finds—
Again the compass tells—
A grey and empty sea.

2.

Turn not away in scorn.
Some day a grave will prove
The frailty of that face,
And worms its grace enjoy.
Let me enjoy you now —
Turn not away in scorn.

3.

All your young beauty is to me
Like a place where the new grass sways,
After the blessing of the rain,
When the sun unveils its light.

Margaret Laurence

Infinite are the types of women:
Is it possible for me to describe them?
By God, I say, I shall make a try.

A woman without a husband,
Even if she be the Sultan's daughter,
Is without modesty;
I know her cunning:
Will one like her be my joy?

A mature girl of many years
With furrowed cheeks
And breasts like little bags of skin:
Will one like her be my joy?

Another with melted butter on her shoulders;
How she stinks,
Her squalor is like poison:
Will one like her be my joy?

Another is short,
She waddles about
And has an ugly look,
Her squalor is like garbage:
I am not drawn to her.

Another has scrawny shoulders
And resembles an ostrich
With its feet bound:
Will one like her be my joy?

But there is one,
The fame of her beauty cries out louder
Than camels preening themselves at the wells of Bullala,
Than children singing songs in front of the King's relatives,
Or than wise men raising their voices before beginning a
     pilgrimage to Mecca;
Her fame is spread by every ship;
Also she was born in high position:
Will one like her be my joy?

Her hips are admirably separated from her thin waist,
Hers are beautiful thighs and swinging hands,
Her hair is silken, her nose admirable,
Her teeth are like white wool.
O righteous Lord, finally give me
This beauty I have chosen.

Enrico Cerulli

The best dance is the dance of the Eastern clans,
The best people are ourselves,
Of this I have always been sure.
The best wealth is camels,
The *duur* grass is the best fresh grazing,
The *dareemo* grass is the best hay,
Of this I have always been sure.

B. Andrzejewski and I. M. Lewis

Lullaby

Somba

If your mother has set out to fish,
I shall watch over you,
For she will give me a prawn.
If your mother has gone to crush corn,
I shall watch over you,
For she will give me a share of the pudding.
But if your mother has sallied forth to drink,
I shall abandon you to the ants,
For upon her return she will be tipsy
And not think about me.

*Ch. Béart**

Song of Novices in the Secret
Society of Snake Charmers

Sukuma

Whoever looks at us with envy
May become blind.
Whoever pursues us
Who are joining the Society,
May die;
He will burst like clouds.

Hans Cory

I have given up singing about men,
I am looking only for clouds,
The millet has withered in the field.
The world has gone from bad to worse,
We die like fools.

Rest under a tree and you rise no more.
By God, some day or other
Clouds appear and you say,
Perhaps it will rain today.
But the sun takes its walk through the sky,
And no rain comes down, not even a little,
To drive us into shelter.

When the sky is absolutely clear these days,
Even a fool then knows
That the world is undone.

Hans Koritschoner

The European   *Sukuma*

I feel cuts in my heart
As if done with a razor.
I have an enemy, who is stronger than I;
My heart is gloomy.

My enemy in this struggle is the stronger,
He has eyes like a pouncing cat
Which has missed its mouse:
I cannot resist.

Hans Koritschoner

A Ditty   *Swahili*

A fetter and a chain:
Love is sweet
To those who love each other;
But unrequited love is poison
Which slays like madness.

A. Werner

Let me ask: for what reason or rhyme
Do women refuse to marry?
Woman cannot exist except by man:
What is there in that
To vex some of them so?
A woman is she who has a husband —
Then she cannot but prosper.

Lyndon Harries

The Poor Man *Swahili*

The face of a poor man is furrowed
By hunger and thirst
That is in his vitals.
Poverty is no state fit for mortal man:
It makes him a beast
To be fed upon grass.
Poverty is not right:
When a man gets it,
Though he be nobly born,
He has no power with God.

Lyndon Harries

I dwell not in the city to become a worthless object,
I go into the forest to be eaten by the alien.
If the alien seizes me and devours my flesh,
So be it: to be killed by the enemy is the fortune of war.
A nobleman is like an elephant: he does not die in bed,
But by the keen-edged sword which kills in battle.
A nobleman is a spitting cobra: he dies hard.

Lyndon Harries

Lullaby

Be quiet, my baby,
Be still, my child,
Your mother has gone to get green mealies,
Your sisters are all gone gathering wood,
So be quiet, baby, be still.
Your father has gone awalking,
He has gone to drink good beer,
Your mother is working with a will,
So be quiet, baby, be still.

E. J. Bourhill and J. B. Drake

Even when she does not look up,
She has a lovely neck;
Even when she is not stretching,
She has beautiful hips;
Her hair is full,
Her neck slender,
Her eyelashes black,
Her eyes white,
Her gums green,
Her teeth bright,
Her belly small,
Her hands soft.

Fatima, the clever one,
When I do not see her,
Bitterness slays my eyes;
When she does not speak,
Bitterness slays my ears.
Because of Fatima, the clever one,
Cold slays me in the evening,
Heat devours me in the morning.
I have filled my heart with words;
So many tears flow out of my eyes
That I scatter holes upon the sand.

To one who is possessed you refuse a cure,
To one who is ill you deny recovery.
Fatima, clever one, say "come,"
And I shall come in haste;
Say "don't come,"
And I shall come anyway.

*Johannes Lukas**

Praise for a Chief   *Tembu*

See how the doves flutter and huddle,
Dismayed at the sight of the eagle:
Woe to the dove that has no wings.

A. C. Jordan

Concerning the Totemic
Animal of an Age Group

The lion kills and keeps,
The lion kills and keeps.
He kills the giraffe and keeps,
The lion kills and keeps.
The animals gather,
Mine is the tawny one.
He kills the hartebeest and keeps,
He kills the eland and keeps,
The zebra and keeps, the giraffe and keeps;
He kills the buffalo;
He kills the waterbuck, the curved-horned animal.
We sing his praises.
Let us stand and spear the lion
With our spear and kill it.

J. C. D. Lawrance

Complaint of a Jilted Lover   *Thonga*

Refuse me if you will, girl.
The grains of maize you eat in your village are human eyes,
The tumblers from which you drink are human skulls,
The manioc roots you eat are human tibia,
The sweet potatoes are human fingers.
Refuse me, if you will, girl.

Henri A. Junod

Thonga

Song of Young Men Working
in Gold Mines of Johannesburg

Stones are very hard to break
Far from home, in a foreign land,
Far from home, in a foreign land,
Stones are very hard to break.

Henri A. Junod

Prayer of Warriors

I am sharpening my sword:
O High God, if you wish
You may give me
What you wish.
What will fall in front of me
Is what you give me.
What you do not give me
I cannot find.

Günter Wagner

Love Song of a Girl

The far-off mountains hide you from me,
While the nearer ones overhang me.
Would that I had a heavy sledge
To crush the mountains near me.
Would that I had wings like a bird
To fly over those farther away.

A. C. Jordan

Taunts of Old Women
to a Pregnant Wife

Yao

First you sought pleasure,
Now you will have pain instead;
You will no longer have your beauty,
For you are not a girl any more
But a child's mother.

While you ate, it was sweet,
But now it is sour:
Nasty, nasty, nasty.
Both day and night
It was your custom to sleep together:
Nasty, nasty, nasty.

A. M. Hokororo

It is what befits you that gives you dignity.
A rope on its neck in no way befits a fowl.
Three ears do not at all befit the head.
Shorts and jacket, both combined in a garb,
Do not indeed befit a human being;
Such a garment becomes either slack or tight.
A self-respecter always sees to it
That whatever clothing he puts on
Fits fine, exactly and impeccably.

A deaf man, a blind man, or a lame man,
Does not in any way befit the throne.
For cleaning nostrils, the finger we use
Is always that befitting the nose.

The power of ordering culprits to be killed
Is granted to an Oba, not because
He likes drinking human blood now and then,
But just to give him greater dignity.

When a group of boys, girls, men, or wives,
Go together in a happy company,
Dignity attends them in every step.
As a pigeon always has dignity,
And as a turtledove is nowhere ill at ease,
So, with an unblemished heart, may you be.

E. A. Babalola

Moral Discourses
of the Supreme God

1.

The corn in the farm bows before the wind,
And a light breeze after rain
Causes the leaves of the little trees
To droop.
If a boy salutes his father,
Everything he does will prosper;
His behavior will be quiet and well-ordered.
If a wife honors her husband,
She will rejoice.

2.

The whole world seeks
Good things for itself.
If mine be good,
May yours be good.
It is only another
Who wishes you harm,
Not yourself.

3.

If we want to tell a lie,
Our eyes will be insistent and shifty.
If we want to tell the truth,
Our body will be quiet and peaceful.
A lie cannot be told face to face.

J. D. Clarke

Praise Songs for Eshu Elegba,
the God of Mischief

1.

His teeth grinding like stones,
He comes out bringing his club.
He is the one who fights,
He is the one who bears a club,
He is the smooth-haired one,
The one with hair down the back of his head,
The one with fullness of hair.
Elegba, the strong man, is coming.

2.

He of the 1600 clubs
Staggers about,
He puts a club in the hands of quarrelers.

3.

If he has left his cloth behind,
He carries off cloth from the cloth seller.
If he leaves his wife behind,
Husbands must go searching for their wives.

4.

We are singing for the sake of Eshu,
He used his penis to make a bridge:
The penis broke in two,
The travelers fell into the river.

Joan Wescott

Ziba   Maiden's Song

I refused, of course I did,
I do not want to get married.
But father and mother compel me to,
And so I am willing to give it a try.

*Hermann Rehse**

Ziba   War Song

You sought firewood and fire
At the grave of the priest:
That does not matter in the least.

*Hermann Rehse**

Zulu   Modern Concert Song

Come here, my beloved,
Come, give me a kiss.
There is a new law
Which says we must embrace each other.

Hugh Tracey

Love Song

Wherever I go,
I wish to go with you, my beloved.
I can see nothing to keep us apart.
Whenever I think,
I think of you.
I can see nothing to keep us apart, my beloved.
My heart is comforted by you, my beloved.

Hugh Tracey

Song of Those Growing Old

Zulu

The body perishes, the heart stays young.
The platter wears away with serving food.
No log retains its bark when old,
No lover is peaceful while the rival weeps.

Hugh Tracey

References

(The precise page on which a poem appears in each reference is indicated in parentheses; the pages on which the entire article appears are placed outside the parentheses. Unless otherwise noted, the poem from a French- or German-language reference has been translated by the editor of this volume.)

Adali-Mortti, Geormbeeyi. "Ewe Poetry." *Black Orpheus*, 1958, no. 4, pp. 36-45 (p. 42, Ewe: Yearning).

Andrzejewski, B. W. and Lewis, I. M. *Somali Poetry.* Oxford: Clarendon Press, 1964 (p. 144; Somali; Traditional Song).

Arnott, D. W. "Proverbial Lore and Word-Play of the Fulani." *Africa*, 1957, v. 27, pp. 379-96 (p. 393, Fulani: A Chain-Rhyme).

Babalola, E. A. "New Yoruba Poems." *African Affairs*, 1954, v. 53, pp. 332-37 (pp. 334-35, Yoruba: Dignity).

Béart, Ch. "Jeux et jouets de l'ouest Africain." *Mémoires de l'Institut Français d'Afrique Noire*, 1955, no. 1 (p. 65, Basari: Lullaby; p. 68, Somba: Lullaby).

Bleek, Dorothea F. "Bushman Folklore." *Africa*, 1929, v. 2, pp. 302-13 (p. 307, Bushmen: Prayer to the Star Canopus).

Bourhill, E. J. and Drake, J.B. *Fairy Tales From South Africa.* London: Macmillan, 1908 (p. 71, Swazi: Lullaby).

Bowdich, T. Edward. *Mission from Cape Coast Castle to Ashantee.* London: John Murray, 1819 (p. 369, Ashanti: Antiphony).

Campbell, Dugald. *In the Heart of Bantuland.* London: Seeley, Service, 1922 (p. 129, Central Bantu: Song for the Lazy).

Cendrars, Blaise. *The African Saga*. New York: Payson and Clarke, 1927 (p. 315, Maasai: Proverb; p. 347, Maasai: Song to a Gun; pp. 351-52, Pygmies: Dance of the Animals; translated by Margery Bianco).

Cerulli, Enrico. "Somali Songs and Little Texts." *Journal of the African Society*, 1919, v. 19, pp. 135-40; 1920, v. 19, pp. 221-26; 1920, v. 20, pp. 46-49 (v. 19, p. 140, Somali: A Boast of the Mad Mullah Who Fought the British; v. 20, p. 48, Somali: Species of Women).

Christaller, J. G. 'Twi Mmebusem Mpensa-Ahansia Mmoaano." *In* J. B. Danquah, *The Akan Doctrine of God*. London: Lutterworth Press, 1944 (p. 193, Akan: Evaluation).

Clarke, J. D. "Ifa Divination." *Journal of the Royal Anthropological Institute*, 1939, v. 69, pp. 235-56 (pp. 248-49, Yoruba: Moral Discourses of the Supreme God).

Corey, Hans. "The Buyeye." *Africa*, 1946, v. 16, pp. 160-78 (p. 169, Sukuma: Song of Novices in the Secret Society of Snake-Charmers).

Danquah, J. B. *Akan Laws and Customs*. London: Routledge, 1928 (p. 252, Akan: A Song of the Minstrels).

Delobsom, A. A. Dim. *L'empire du Mogho-Naba*. Paris: Loviton, 1932 (p. 234, Mossi: Songs During Love Dances; translated by Kathryn A. Looney for the Human Relations Area Files).

Dempwolff, Otto. *Die Sandawe*. Hamburg: L. Friederichsen, 1916 (p. 174, Sandawe: Song for a Dance).

Driberg, J. H. *The Lango*. London: T. Fisher Unwin, 1923 (pp. 250-51, Lango: Rain-Making Litany; pp. 255-58, Lango: Songs for the Rain Festival).

———————————————— *People of the Small Arrow*. New York: Payson & Clarke, 1930 (p. 38, Acholi: Battle Hymn; p. 44, Didinga: Hymn of Propitiation; p. 323, Didinga: Song for Dance of Young Girls).

Ebding, Friedrich and Ittmann, Johannes. "Religiöse Gesänge aus dem nördlichen Waldland von Kamerun." *Afrika und Uebersee*, 1955, v. 39, pp. 169-78; v. 40, pp. 39-44; 1956, v. 40, pp. 125-32 (pp. 40-41, Duala: Funeral Hymns).

Eiselen, W. M. "The Art of Divination as Practised by the Bama-semola." *Bantu Studies*, 1932, v. 6, pp. 1-29 (pp. 15, 18, 21, 22, 27, Masemola: Formulas Recited as Divinations After

Throwing Four Principal and Forty-Two Accessory Bones).

Ennis, Merlin. *Umbundu: Folk Tales From Angola.* Boston: Beacon Press, 1962 (p. 315, Mbundu: Preoccupation).

Esser, Joseph. *Légende Africaine.* Paris: Presses de la Cité, 1957 (pp. 117, 167, 188, 213, Mongo: From the Legend of the National Hero).

Field, M. J. *Religion and Medicine of the Ga People.* London: Oxford University Press, 1961 (p. 172, Ga: Blessings Upon an Infant).

Fosbrooke, H. A. "A Rangi Circumcision Ceremony." *Tanganyika Notes and Records,* 1958, no. 50, pp. 30-38 (p. 35, Rangi: Song During Circumcision Rites).

Gutmann, Bruno. *Dichten und Denken der Dschagganeger.* Leipzig: Evang.-Luth. Mission, 1909 (pp. 22-23, Chaga: Tributes to the Chief).

------------------------------. "Kinderspiele bei den Wadschagga." *Globus,* 1909, v. 95, pp. 300-304 (p. 303, Chaga: Children's Song).

------------------------------. *Das Dschaggaland und seine Christen.* Leipzig: Evang.-Luth. Mission, 1925 (p. 23, Chaga: Morning Prayer).

Hambly, Wilfrid Dyson. "Occupational Ritual, Belief, and Custom Among the Ovimbundu." *American Anthropologist,* 1934, v. 36, pp. 157-67 (p. 160, Mbundu: Song of the Fishermen).

Harries, Lyndon. *Swahili Poetry.* Oxford: Clarendon, 1962 (p. 146, Swahili: The Poor Man; p. 148, Swahili: The Warrior; p. 185, Swahili: In Praise of Marriage).

Herskovits, Frances. "Dahomean Songs." *Poetry,* 1934, v. 40, pp. 75-77 (p. 75, Dahomeans: Song to the Envious).

------------------------------. "Dahomean Songs for the Dead." *New Republic,* 1935, v. 84, p. 95 (p. 95, Dahomeans: Dirge).

Herskovits, Melville J. *Dahomey.* New York: Augustin, 1938, Vol. I (p. 275, Dahomeans: Ditty for a Child Losing His First Tooth; p. 343, Dahomeans: Chorus Sung by Co-Wives to One Another; translated by Frances Herskovits).

Hokororo, A. M. "The Influence of the Church on Tribal Customs at Lukuledi." *Tanganyika Notes and Records,* 1960, no. 54, pp. 1-13 (pp. 5, 6, Yao: Taunts of Old Women to a Pregnant Wife).

Honeÿ, James A. *South-African Folk-Tales*. New York: Baker and Taylor, 1910 (p. 138, Bushmen: The Sun's Curse Upon the Horse).

Ittmann, Johannes. *In* Friedrich Ebding and Johannes Ittmann (*quod vide*) (p. 125, Duala: Song).

Jordan, A. C. "Towards an African Literature: II. Traditional Poetry." *Africa South*, 1957, v. 2, no. 1, pp. 97-105 (p. 99, Hlubi: Girl's Song; p. 99, Xhosa: Love Song of a Girl; p. 105, Tembu: Praise for a Chief).

Joslin, Mike. *Märchen von der Goldküste*. Munich; Nymphenburger Verlagshandlung, 1960 (p. 178, Ghanaians: Song of the Turtle).

Junod, Henri A. *The Life of a South African Tribe*. London: Macmillan, 1927. Vol. II (p. 191, Thonga: Complaint of a Jilted Lover; p. 284, Thonga: Song of Young Men Working in Gold Mines of Johannesburg).

Kagwa, Apolo. *The Customs of the Baganda*. New York: Columbia University Press, 1934 (p. 141, Ganda: In Honor of a King Who Acquired Several Young Wives; translated by Ernest B. Kalibala).

Kidney, Ella. "Native Songs from Nyasaland." *Journal of the African Society*, 1920, v. 20, pp. 116-26 (p. 126, Nyasa Peoples: Lament).

Koritschoner, Hans. "Some East African Native Songs." *Tanganyika Notes and Records*, 1937, no. 4, pp. 51-64 (p. 55, Sukuma: The European; p. 59, Nyamwezi: Hunter's Song; p. 62, Sukuma: The Drought; p. 64, Ngoni: Dance Tune).

Koshland, Miriam. "The Poetry of Madagascar." *Africa South*, 1960, v. 4, no. 2, pp. 114-22 (p. 117, Malagasy: Hain-Teny).

Laurence, Margaret. *A Tree for Poverty*. Nairobi, Kenya: Eagle Press, 1954 (pp. 31, 33, Somali: Love Lyrics).

Lawrance, J. C. D. *The Itesco*. London: Oxford University Press, 1957 (p. 81, Tesco: Concerning the Totemic Animal of an Age Group).

Lebzelter, Vicktor. *Eingeborenenkulturen in Südwest- und Südafrika*. Leipzig: Hiersemann, 1934 (p. 75, Bushmen: Hunting Prayer; translated by Richard Neuse for the Human Relations Area Files).

Leslau, Wolf. "The Farmer in Chaha Song." *Africa,* 1964, v. 34, pp. 230-42 (pp. 231-32, Gurage: The Farmer).

Lienhardt, Godfrey. *Divinity and Experience.* Oxford, Clarendon, 1961 (p. 282, Dinka: War Song).

Little, K. L. " A Mende Musician Sings of His Adventures." *Man,* 1948, v. 48, pp. 27-28 (p. 27, Mende: Minstrel's Song).

Lukas, Johannes. "Tubu-Texte und Uebungsstücke." *Afrika und Uebersee,* 1953/54, v. 38, pp. 1-16, 53-68, 121-34 (p. 56, Teda: To Fatima).

Merwe, D. F. v. d. "Hurutshe Poems." *Bantu Studies,* 1941, v. 15, pp. 307-37 (p. 334, Hurutshe: To Doves).

Migeod, F. W. H. *The Mende Language.* London: Kegan Paul, Trench, Trübner, 1908 (p. 270, Mende: On Wealth).

Nketia, J. H. Kwabena. "West African Voices." *African Affairs,* 1949, v. 48, pp. 156-58 (p. 157, Akan: Elegy for Duodu, a Brave Man).

————————————————————. "Akan Poetry." *Black Orpheus,* 1958, no. 3, pp. 5-27 (p. 18, Akan: Cradle Songs).

————————————————————. *Folk Songs of Ghana.* Legon: University of Ghana, 1963 (p. 29, Akan: Song for an Absent Chief; pp. 37, 57, Akan: Love Songs; p. 79, Akan: Dancing Song).

Nyabongo, Akiki K. *The Story of an African Chief.* New York: Scribner's, 1935 (p. 185, Ganda: Maternal Advice to Young Parrots).

Osadebay, D. C. "West African Voices." *African Affairs,* 1949, v. 48, pp. 151-54 (pp. 153-54, Ibo: Love Song for Nneka).

Pankhurst, Sylvia. *Ethiopia.* Essex: Lalibela House, 1959 (pp. 416-17, Amhara: Household Song).

Patterson, J. R. *Kanuri Songs.* Lagos, Nigeria: Government Printer, 1926 (pp. 1, 2, 8, 9, 10, 17, 23, 27, 31, Kanuri: Praise Songs for Various Chiefs and Sultans; p. 18, Kanuri: On Truth).

Peristiany, J. G. *The Social Institutions of the Kipsigis.* London: Routledge & Kegan Paul; New York: Humanities Press Inc., 1939 (pp. 264-66, Kipsigi: Army Song; pp. 272-73,, Kipsigi:

Girls' Secret Love Song).

Prietze, Rudolf. "Dichtung der Haussa." *Africa,* 1931, v. 4, pp. 86-95 (p. 94, Hausa: Wail of One Rejected).

Ranaivo, Flavien. "Der Madegasse im Spiegel von Sprach und Heimat." *Afrika Heute,* 1962, pp. 52-61 (p. 59, Malagasy: A Love Message).

Rattray, R. S. *"Some Folk-Lore Stories and Songs in Chinyanja."* London: Society for Promoting Christian Knowledge, 1907 (p. 119, Nyanja: Prayer for Rain).

--. *Ashanti Proverbs.* Oxford: Clarendon, 1916 (p. 25, Ashanti: Perspective).

--. *Religion and Art in Ashanti.* Oxford: Clarendon, 1927 (p. 73, Ashanti: Chant for Girls During Puberty Ceremony).

Read, Margaret. "Songs of the Ngoni People" *Bantu Studies,* 1937, v. 11, pp. 1-35 (p. 4, Ngoni: Lullaby; pp. 14-15, Ngoni: Litany).

Rehse, Hermann. *Kizibia: Land und Leute.* Stuttgart: Strecker & Schröder, 1910 (p. 72, Ziba: War Song; p. 73, Ziba: Maiden's Song).

Richards, Audrey I. *Chisungu.* London: Faber & Faber, 1956 (p. 198, Bemba: Initiation Song of Girls).

Schapera, I. "Premarital Pregnancy and Native Opinion." *Africa,* 1933, v. 6, pp. 59-89 (p. 74, Kgatla: Lullaby of an Abandoned Mother).

--. *Praise-Poems of Tswana Chiefs.* Oxford: Clarendon, 1965 (p. 161, Ngwaketse: Praise for a Chief).

Schultze, Leonhard. *Aus Namaland und Kalahari.* Jena: Gustav Fischer, 1907 (p. 379, Hottentots: Civil War Song; p. 382, Hottentots: Love Song).

Smith, Mary. *Baba of Karo.* London: Faber & Faber, 1954 (pp. 57-58, Hausa: Praise Song for a Drummer).

Somali Ministry of Information. *(Poster promoting tourism).* Mogadishu: Government Printing Office, 1965 (Somalia: Legend).

Stefaniszyn, B. "The Hunting Songs of the Ambo." *African Studies,* 1951, v. 10, pp. 1-12 (pp. 5, 8, 9, 10, Ambo: Hunting Songs).

Tessmann, Günter. *Die Pangwe*. Berlin: Ernst Wasmuth, 1913. Vol. II (p. 313, Fang: Distracting an Opponent in a Game of Skill; translated by Richard Neuse for the Human Relations Area Files).

Tracey, Hugh. *"Lalela Zulu": 100 Zulu Lyrics*. Johannesburg: African Music Society, 1948 (p. 22, Zulu: Song of Those Growing Old; p. 36, Zulu: Love Song; p. 59, Zulu: Modern Concert Song).

--, "The Social Role of African Music." *African Affairs*, 1954, v. 53, pp. 234-41 (p. 238, Hima: Song).

Trilles, R. P. H. "Le totémisme chez les Fân." *Bibliothéque Anthropos*, 1912, v. 1, no. 4 (p. 539, Fang: Invocation to the Spirit of the Race; translated by Isabell Athey for the Human Relations Area Files).

Vergiat, A. M. *Les rites secrets primitifs de l'Oubangui*. Paris: Payot, 1936 (pp. 85, 90, Bangi: Songs During Circumcision Rites; pp. 107-8, Bangi: Songs before Clitoridectomy Rites).

Wagner, Günter. *The Bantu of North Kavirondo*. London: Oxford University Press, 1949. Vol. I (p. 171, Vugushu: Prayer of Warriors; p. 294, Logoli: Prayer to Ancestral Spirits).

Warner, Esther. *Seven Days to Lomaland*. Boston: Houghton Mifflin, 1954 (p. 180, Loma: Mothers' Song).

Werner, A. "Native Poetry in East Africa." *Africa*, 1928, v. 1, pp. 348-57 (pp. 352-53, Swahili: A Ditty).

Wescott, Joan. "The Sculpture and Myths of Eshu Elegba, the Yoruba Trickster." *Africa*, 1962, v. 32, pp. 336-54 (pp. 337, 343, 344, Yoruba: Praise Songs for Eshu Elegba, the God of Mischief).

Westermann, Diedrich. *A Study of the Ewe Language*. London: Oxford University Press, 1930 (p. 249, Ewe: Dolor).

Wiegräbe, Paul. Ewelieder. *Afrika und Uebersee*, 1953, v. 37, pp. 99-108; 1953, v. 38, pp. 17-26; 1954, v. 38, pp. 113-120, 155-64 (v. 37, pp. 101, 102, 103, Ewe: Complaints; v. 38, p. 17, Ewe: The Sorrows of Death).

Wing, J. Van. *Études Bakongo*. Bruges: Desclée de Brouwer, 1959 (p. 137, Kongo: Hymn to God; pp. 442-43, Kongo: Incantation During Initiation into a Secret Society).